transparency

John Kim, LMFT

PREFACE

I've never considered myself a writer. I lack vocabulary and if it wasn't for my patient editor, this entire book would be one long run-on sentence. The birth of *Transparency* was due to two events in my life. One: working as a therapist in residential treatment. Two: my blog.

For four years I treated teenagers struggling with substance abuse in a residential setting. I begrudgingly went to work every day in khakis and a dark blue Polo shirt (the uniform). I escorted kids on outings, went grocery shopping, and ran groups. I felt more like a camp counselor than a therapist. It's not what I had in mind when I decided to go back to school at thirty-something to become a therapist. But through this experience, I learned about a treatment model called Therapeutic Community. It's the idea that we can rebuild ourselves through others. I applied some of those concepts in my own life while going through a divorce. Through this experience, I came up with my own method. Meanwhile, I created a blog to spark a dialogue to help others. The process of sharing my journey and helping people with theirs gave me something I've never had before. A purpose.

There were two things I needed for this book to happen: a message and courage. Working in Therapeutic Community gave me my method - my message. The love and support I received, and all the inspirational stories I was able to be a part of through my blog, gave me the courage.

ACKNOWLEDGEMENTS

I want to thank all my followers on my blog, everyone who's ever asked me a question, shared a story, or given me words of encouragement. My parents and brother for their unconditional love and support. Crossfit Hollywood for helping me crush false beliefs about myself and showing me that transformation is possible if you just put the work in. I want to thank all the kids and families I treated in residential. The staff and clients I work with at Oceanside in Malibu. Aubrey Hicks, for editing my little book. Padhia Avocado, for all your amazing artwork and support. You're a true gift. Anyone who has allowed me to be a part of your journey, thank you. You guys have taught me how to be transparent and the true meaning of working on oneself.

A supervisor once told me that "you will only be one point in someone's journey, so just be a bright one."

Thank you guys for being bright points in *my* journey.

This book is for those who don't like self help books.

Self help books are like bacon; they have a lot of fat. They're greasy, slippery, and easy to forget. My goal in writing this was to create one with less slip and more stick. Straight to the point. Less poetry, more practicality This book is only three chapters. It's meant to be read in one sitting, on any platform, web, screen, phone, or paper. It's meant to be carried with you; in your device, your purse, or your back pocket. It is a reminder, a check list, and a guide.

Use it when you need it.

My Method

When people ask what I do for a living, I tell them I build containers. I believe most of us have cracked containers. Cracks come from abusive relationships, dysfunctional families, our life experiences (situational or relational), that have caused us some version of trauma or pain. Cracked containers prevent growth. It doesn't matter if you're going through a painful breakup, struggling with an addiction, or fighting an eating disorder. A safe container will allow you to maneuver through life easier. It will protect you and promote growth. My goal in writing this book is to give you tools to build a new safe container for yourself.

Therapists tend to be very private people, which means we do not disclose. It's not our fault. Textbooks drilled it into our heads in grad school. Our degrees slapped us with a very firm sense of should and should not. I am here to break confidentiality and turn labels on their heads.

They say that before you write a screenplay, you must know all the rules of story telling: you must study the masters that have come before you, you must study structure, act breaks, etc. . Once you have learned the rules and studied the masters -- toss everything out the window and come up with your own style. I apply this concept as a therapist. I have studied all the theoretical orientations from Psychodynamic to Narrative, Existential to Strategic, Family Systems to Cognitive Behavioral, and I do pull from them. I also have my own style.

I believe in transparency. I believe it is important that you know who I am in order for you to trust me with your story. I believe in *with* you not *at* you. Many self help books are distant, speak in third person, and don't give real life examples. I would like to bring you close, use I statements, and give examples from my own life. So as you read this book you will not only know how I work, you will also know who I am.

Let's begin.

My method is very simple. It's broken down into three stages.

TRANSPARENCY
STANCE
CONTAINER

In Transparency, you are softening the soil. This is preparation. It requires a decision to be raw. You will feel vulnerable and naked, but you must push through. The ground must be tilled. If you can't commit to this stage, you will not have the tools to move on to the next. In Stance, you are planting seeds. You are driving your stake, building your fence, envisioning your garden. In Container, you are allowing growth, baring fruit. Continuing to work all three stages will be the water and sun that keeps you growing and maneuvering at your highest potential.

Chapter One

TRANSPARENCY

It all starts here. In order to build a safe container you must have the ability to communicate your state, your soul, your truth. In order to do that, you need strong transparency muscles. Yes, muscles. I believe your ability to be honest, with yourself and others, is like a muscle in that the more you exercise it, the stronger it will get.

If You Died Tomorrow

I spent my 20s in the corner of dark coffee shops, desperately beating my brain for snappy dialogue and seamless act breaks, all to sell the million-dollar screenplay. It was my ticket into the quad, where cheerleaders and football players talk about parties and prom, the address of "The American Dream." If at that time someone asked me, *If you died tomorrow, would you feel okay with your contributions on earth?* I would have said *no* without any hesitation. I was a starving writer. My life hadn't even begun yet. It was on hold, *I* was on hold, until I had a house in the hills, a three picture deal, and my own office on a studio lot. Although I had sold a couple of scripts, there was no real contribution, only words on a shelf and a desperate desire to chase a rainbow made of Coca Cola.

Recently, I asked myself the same question: *If I died tomorrow, would I feel okay with my contribution on earth?*

The last five years of my life flashed by like a film stuck in fast forward. Rapid montages stamped with faces of all the kids and families I've been treating; their tears, their smiles, and their laughter echoed. Then I saw all the people in my personal life; the authentic friendships I've made, and their unconditional love for someone with nothing to offer but a worn heart and a dull ear.

The people I've been helping on my blog, through emails, questions, webcam sessions, through hearing amazing stories, hopes, dreams, revelations, and the privilege I've had to be a part of all that, is what makes me say, *Yes, I would feel okay.* I don't have a mansion, a book deal, or a private practice in Malibu. I'm a guy with a blog. But, it's the first time in my life I feel I like I've made a contribution in this world.

It took a family business, marriage, and my own personal growth to finally have the courage and tools to redefine what is valuable, meaningful, and worth fighting for. It required being okay with me and my defects and knowing what I have to offer. I couldn't have done this without being transparent, creating a stance, and building my own safe container.

Ask yourself, *If you died tomorrow, are you okay with your contributions? Is your work done here on earth? Do you have anything else to give?*

Every day that goes by is another chance to leave something behind, to move, teach, support, encourage, entertain, help, raise, invent, define, create, and change.

If your container is cracked, your potential goes down. The chances of you achieving what you were meant to achieve, affect who you were meant to affect, diminishes significantly. Cracked containers allow dysfunction which leads to anxiety and sucks motivation and keeps you stuck in quicksand. What's left is you going through the motions of life but not really living. You become a zombie, a grayed out version of yourself.

dysfunction → anxiety = quicksand

It's time to build yourself a new container.

Solid As Water

People with weak transparency muscles live within a Pseudo Self. In plain English, this is a false version of you. It seeks other people's approval. You live in Pseudo Self because it gives you a sense of security. It allows you to hide and live in disguise. But most importantly, the Pseudo Self straps a muzzle on your gifts. By gifts, I don't necessarily mean talents. I mean what makes you different than any other person on the planet. In screenwriting, they say what's most important is your voice. Everyone has a story to tell, but it's your voice that makes your script stand out from the rest. For example, Quentin Tarantino has a very strong voice. It comes out in his dialogue and his non-linear way of storytelling. Being transparent allows you to find your voice. Your voice is your gift. Your voice is your Solid Self, the true you. What prevents people from exercising their transparency muscle is fear. This fear prevents growth. You must shatter fear or you'll snap back every time you stretch. A good way to remember Pseudo vs Solid is False vs Truth. Pseudo is false. Solid is truth. Everyone has a true and false version of themselves. Many times where we pull from depends on our environment and who we're around. For example, if we're surrounded by people we want to impress, we tend to project an idea of what we believe they are looking for or attracted to. Our dial is turned on Take instead of Give. We are seeking something from them, attention, validation, approval. In order to turn that dial back to Give, we must pull from our truth. We must be transparent in voice and self. This adds solidity. What we are giving is our true self. Everything false clouds the picture of our true self and transparency cuts through the clouds.

In order to live your truth, you must be transparent. You must be clear and flow like liquid. Like Bruce Lee said, *be like water.*

Transparency means finding your voice, being a true version of yourself, and turning your dial to Give.

The Power of a Sandwich

Once I bought someone a sandwich.

I was getting a quick dinner at a local deli when I noticed an older gentleman sitting by himself. He was just sitting there, bobbing his head to the Muzak. He didn't look homeless. He just looked lonely. We made eye contact and he nodded. I quickly turned back to my book, shoved the rest of my sandwich into my mouth, and thought to myself *Maybe I should buy him something to eat.* That thought was my Solid Self - my instinct, my gut, my truth-speaking. He had a soft tone. I could barely hear him. Then my Pseudo Self kicked in, a loud thundering voice that convinced me that the man didn't need a sandwich. Pseudo came at me like a lawyer, logical and cold. *What if he's just waiting for someone? He would be insulted if I asked him if I could buy him food. Maybe he's the owner?*

But these were just excuses to stay in my comfort zone. I finished my sandwich and was about to leave when I stopped myself and thought, *Wait a minute. This isn't about him. This is about me. If I leave, I am allowing the part of me that was formed by abuse, failed relationships, dysfunctional family dynamics, all the shit that's happened to me in life that's lowered my self worth and security, to control me.* All this, just because I wouldn't buy someone a sandwich?

It's not about the sandwich.

It's about allowing your voice to be heard, giving yourself permission to be the true version of you, before life slapped on a veneer. If I leave, I add glue to the beautiful fake porcelain smile. If turn back and go with my initial gut, I may crack that veneer. My dial turned, as did I. I bought the man a sandwich. My Solid Self was happy when the man smiled and nodded at me. The man allowed his Solid Self voice, when he smiled at a stranger, me. My Solid Self didn't want this to be weird. He wanted to acknowledge connection.

By buying a stranger a sandwich, I allowed my Solid Self to be heard. I drove my stake into the ground and told my Pseudo Self to fuck off. Fuck off for every time he made me critical of myself, for every doubt in my worth, and for allowing others to define me. I left the deli feeling a little more powerful than when I arrived and it had nothing to do with their flatbread. Many of you reading this may think I'm crazy for trying to squeeze so much meaning out of such a simple act. You may be telling yourself *Man, this guy's really reaching.* Make a note of that voice. Recognize it. That is your Pseudo Self.

Transparency means fighting your Pseudo (false) self.

Live Outside of Self

I believe many are depressed because they live a self-centered life. I don't mean a life all about you. I mean doing life in your head. By s*elf*, I mean mind. When you live a life centered in self, you are closed, your thoughts are turned inward, and you are listening to a constant inner dialogue of judgment and criticism. *I'm not good enough, pretty enough, strong enough. I could have done better. I don't deserve* _____. Your world is small.

Unless you come from a perfect family and have had nothing but flawless relationships, your head will play this broken record of judgment or criticism. Of course the volume of the record varies, depending on your story. But we all have this playing inside us. It is quicksand. It starts with a raw emotion, anger, hopelessness, loneliness, despair, sadness, and anxiety. We sink deeper as our raw emotion turns into an emotion driven thought - the broken record. An emotion driven through can be okay – it's when the Pseudo Self drives the mind into a pattern of thought that is contrary to the Solid Self that these thoughts can turn into trouble. Or more accurately, false beliefs. For example, *The world would be better off without me. I'd be better off drinking again. No one understands me. No one loves me. I am worthless. I don't deserve any better than this anyway.* These false beliefs create fear and uncertainty. They keep us locked in our heads. They significantly lower our potential and when our potential is low, so is our ability to seek joy and be happy.

The way you break this record is to get out of your mind (self). Accept your feelings but not the judgmental thoughts behind them. Live in how you feel instead of how you think. Living how you feel doesn't mean to just go around being an emotional person. I am talking about labeling yourself, drawing conclusions from your judgment (living how you think). It's okay to feel lonely. It's not okay to stamp yourself as unloveable.

There's a difference between how you feel and who you are.

For many this is a blurry line. Living outside of self allows us to draw that line with a permanent marker instead of chalk. Separating emotion from thought allows us to be present. The world becomes big. Instead of being in gear all the time, we are in neutral. We are able to focus on what's *happening* to us instead of what has *happened* to us. We are our own toughest critics. In order to mute that critical voice, pull yourself out of your thoughts. Unplug the player. You do that by focusing on the here and now.

Be present. Use your senses. Notice what you see, hear, smell, feel, and breathe. Take in life before life takes you in.

Rehab Chronicles

During group, I had my clients write a letter to their future selves. After they did the assignment, I asked them what that process was like. Many of the girls said they noticed it was much easier to give themselves compliments and encouragement. I asked them *why*. They said it was because writing a letter to a future version of themselves allowed them to separate themselves from self, and to step out of their minds for a minute. I asked them if they would be able to verbalize what they wrote in the letter to themselves in present time, right now, if they were alone in front of a mirror. They all said *no way*.

By shifting their lens and living outside of self, they were able to accept compliments and encouragement more than if they were inside their minds. In group, my clients were able to love themselves more by living outside of self.

Living outside of self doesn't mean living out of touch with your emotions or not living in the moment. By "outside" I mean outside of your head, mind, and thoughts. Your mind is the one that plays tricks. Emotions just are.

Transparency means living outside of your thoughts.

Prove Nothing

Say you're at a party and you find yourself acting a certain way to fit in. That's your false self (Pseudo Self). Stop acting and try to be your true self (Solid

Self), even if that means you'll stick out or run the risk of people not liking you. By doing this, you are exercising your transparency muscle. If you purposely exaggerate the version of yourself, thinking you are being more transparent - you're not. You are actually being false. When you are transparent, you are just being you, in your truest form, at every moment. This is extremely difficult. Think about it. Through out the day, when are you purely just you? I think many of us live different versions of ourselves, depending on where we're at and whom we're around.

The less you seek approval, the more transparent you are. The thing is, you're not the only one in the crowd displaying your Pseudo Self. Others are also. So when you show your Solid Self, people notice. Some will not like it, but some will. You will start to attract people that see you for you. These people are valuable. They will be part of building your new container.

Transparency means stop seeking approval.

Life as a Movie Trailer

It was the first group I was asked to run at my new job as a therapist in a private treatment center for eating disorders. I wasn't supposed to run groups until the next week. I was "in training," which meant enjoying a chicken curry sandwich and a cappuccino in my office as I soaked in how cushy this job was compared to working in non-profit. Suddenly, the head therapist popped his head in and said *we're short.* He wasn't referring to our height. I had to think of an intervention, quick. Although I've literally run hundreds of groups, I felt like this was my first time. What was happening was my Pseudo Self was kicking in. It was trying to get me to doubt my own skills. This fear made me break into the treatment center's interventions file. These exercises were proven to work. It was my way of being safe. I found one called *The Human Knot.* I thought it was appropriate since the group was titled *Experiential.*

Before we executed The Human Knot, I came up with a quick exercise off the top of my head. This would be the appetizer before the main course. Since it was more of an appetizer, I didn't feel like it needed to be a real intervention. But what was really happening was by taking the pressure off to be a good therapist, which meant use what other therapists use, I allowed my true self (Solid Self) to speak. My Solid Self had his own ideas. Here's the intervention he came up with.

Take a minute and imagine all the important events that have happened in your life up to this point. Now, string those scenes together any way you wish and picture your life as a movie trailer. Describe the trailer as if you just saw it and you're telling a best friend about it. Tell us what's happening from a visual stand point, what you literally saw. If there's music, voice over, or dialogue, describe that as well.

I knew this was my Solid Self speaking because it was very John Kim. I love movies. I am a very visual person. I am unrehearsed. The intervention had me written all over it. I know it's my Solid Self speaking when what he says is organic, not forced. You'll know your Solid Self when what it says is organic. You can feel it. It feels like you.

What was just supposed to be an opener ended up being the main act. Using visual imagery to stir up emotions was extremely effective. One girl described a scene where she tried to commit suicide by hanging herself but fell off the chair. It was a dark comedy. She laughed. Another girl saw a scene with in which she was bleeding and couldn't go on. She cried. Another described her most intimate day with her husband. Hers was a romance. The group took on a life of its own. They were swimming. The intervention did what it was supposed to, ignite emotion and create dialogue. For the next hour, we processed what came up and how they felt about it. The members then supported and encouraged each other. They felt less alone, less damaged. They had revelations about themselves and what they wanted to change. Growth was happening. I had built a safe container.

After the movie trailer exercise, I decided to execute "The Human Knot" as planned. They did the exercise but seemed to just go through the motions. A few admitted that they had done it before. Of course they had; it was in the sharing file. At the end of group, I asked which exercise they enjoyed more. Everyone couldn't stop talking about the movie trailer and how much came up for them. The movie trailer exercise was me being transparent. The Human Knot was me trying to be my perception of a "good" therapist.

I did not share this story to brag about the effectiveness of my interventions. The point of this story is to show the difference between operating from a true version of yourself and a false version. The false version is a widget. It is made in a factory created by society. The true version is unique, one of kind. Do you want to be a widget or a work of art?

Whether you're at a party, on a date, grocery shopping, or in a meeting at work, fight your false self. Especially at work. I think that's where we live the most false moments of our lives.

Transparency means go with your gut.

Two Kinds of Time

There are two kinds of time: healthy time and unhealthy time. Healthy time is living in the now. Unhealthy time is living in everything that's not the here and now. We Many of us spend most of our time dwelling on the past or obsessing about the future. We get up in the morning thinking about all the things we need to get done in the day. On the drive to work, we analyze past relationships, our accomplishments, our failures, those expensive shoes we're waiting for to go on sale, the potential raise, our credit card bill, the date last night, the party this weekend. Then at work, more to-dos, rehearsing your presentation in your head, why weyou're gaining weight, losing your hair, why he didn't call, she didn't write, reminding ourselves to stop being a push over, debating what we want for lunch, how to change our parents, talk to our boss, address our lover, and suddenly the day is over. Now we're in bed, replaying the day and where we could have done more. This causes insomnia which means we wake up grouchy as we start our mental machine all over again.

Living in healthy time doesn't mean never reflecting on events from the past or thinking about the future. It just means not dwelling or obsessing. The keyword is balance. If you find that most of your thoughts are about the past or future, you are not living in healthy time. If you are not living in healthy time, you are not living. You are worrying. Again, this is your Pseudo Self kicking in. It won't allow you to accept your story. It reminds you of everything you did wrong and shames you for it. It tells you that you must be better because you are not good enough as you are. It wants you to internalize this and start labeling yourself. It wants you to devalue yourself. Your true self has already accepted your story (everything that's happened till this moment). It encourages you to live in the present. Consciously doing this, forcing yourself to live in healthy time, is exercising your transparency muscle.

Your Pseudo Self wants to know who you are. Or more accurately, who you are not. Your Solid Self wants to know *how* you are. By addressing the Solid version of you, you are exercising your transparency muscle. I think we focus way too much on the product, and not enough on the process. By product, I mean who we want to be. Our mind is set on results mode. Life doesn't happen until we get X, Y, and Z or become X, Y, and Z. By thinking this way, we set ourselves up for a greater fall if there is a remote control car under the tree instead of a shiny red bike. This mindset makes it almost impossible to accept ourselves today. If we can't accept ourselves, how can we be happy? We can't. Having goals is healthy. Striving for something is great. But being in the process instead of enjoying the process is not. This is why I have a problem with *I am a work in progress.* I don't have a problem with the message. I have a problem with the mindset (the mind is set). The mindset tells us that we are not complete until we reach a certain goal, until we become something, someone. Every chapter in our lives is significant and meaningful.

Stop wanting to rip out chapters. Your life is an amazing story. Don't ruin it.

Transparency means living in the here and now.

Take Off Your Bowling Shoes

Every Sunday morning, I sit down with my friend (spiritual mentor, brother) at a local breakfast joint in Silverlake to sip coffee, process life, and inhale chocolate croissants. One morning, he gave me some great advice regarding the anxiety I had been experiencing in a new job. What he said really hit me because it was so simple. He said *don't own it.* I thought about this. Then I thought about it again. He was absolutely right. If I don't own it, it won't own me.

The fight you had with your boyfriend, the date that went south, the transition of a new job, these events are not yours to own. They were a gift from God, the universe, whatever higher power you believe in. They are yours to borrow and learn from.

I think we create anxiety because we clutch on to things, want to control them. We do this with our children, our relationships, our jobs, and ourselves. But if you believe you do not own the event/experience, it won't have power over you. This doesn't mean don't own your feelings. Your feelings are valid and you do own them because they are your truth. But the shit that's happening in your life is separate from you. You are borrowing those experiences like a pair of bowling shoes. You get to use them as tools. Without ownership, there is no urge to control. Get rid of the desire to control and the burden is suddenly lifted.

Transparency means to not own what's not yours.

Live Inside Out

Most of us allow external objects to define us. Money. Career. Cars. Aesthetics. Other people's opinions. With this mindset, it is nearly impossible to be an authentic version of ourselves. We will morph our truth to match these objects and slowly lose our voice and the imprint we're supposed to leave on this world. Instead, the world will leave its mark on us, having power over our thoughts and behavior. We will walk with *shoulds,* compare our story with others, and constantly chase. This process mutes us and sets us up for steep falls. Once we fall we internalize and end up tightening our muzzle. It's impossible to live at our potential when we are muted.

Living inside out also means not holding feelings inside. Trapped feelings turn into anger and resentment. We end up carrying this weight. It hardens our shoulders and makes us slouch. We concave. In order to move through life with a gorilla chest, with certainty and transparency, we must unload what we carry. The treasure is not outside. What makes us valuable is what's within.   If we decide to live inside out, we will share our value with the world.   If we don't, we will not.

Transparency means to live inside out.

Share Your Story

Sharing your story doesn't mean verbally vomiting on someone.   It means being vulnerable and disclosing when appropriate.   You have to define what *appropriate* means for you.   For me, if the desire to share is driven by ego or coming from an attention seeking place, it's probably not appropriate.   If that desire is coming from a place where you think your story will help someone, it's appropriate.   An easy way to determine if sharing is appropriate is if it is giving, it's appropriate.   If it is taking, it's not.   For example, if it comes from seeking validation, it's taking.   If it validates someone else, it is giving.

Sharing your story is a gift.   The act of it is giving. Giving is being transparent.   Say you were at that same party we discussed before, and learned that someone was going through a divorce.   She admitted it to the group of single people you were chatting with.   The discussion was about how difficult it is to find *good honest friends in this town.*   Since her divorce, she has not been able to find new friends.   It was courageous of her to disclose this since society tends to stamp *defective* on your forehead when you are divorced.   Say you are also going through a divorce.   If you decide to share your story, you are giving.   You are giving someone support. You are the person that will be valuable in her new container.

We learn more from other people's stories than we do our own. If no one shared their stories, where would we be? What lessons would we learn? How alone would we feel?

We are all a million walking stories. Your story is what makes you *you*. Your Pseudo Self will want you to close your book. Your Solid Self will want you to open it.

Transparency means to accept, embrace, and share your story.

The Magic Moment

INT. THERAPY ROOM - DAY (2003-ish)

JOHN sits in front of his THERAPIST, a silver haired man in his 50's sporting a wrinkle free shirt and a bright tie.

> THERAPIST
> How was this week?

> JOHN
> Instead of talking about that, can we talk about my career?

> THERAPIST
> Sure.

> JOHN
> I don't know if I want to pursue it anymore.

> THERAPIST

Why not?

                    JOHN
Sitting in coffee shops all day writing dialogue
and trying to come up with the next big idea
isn't as exciting as it once was. I'm sick of being
a starving artist. It's affecting my marriage.
Also, I feel like I'm getting older.

                  THERAPIST
     You are not a starving artist. You've sold
  scripts. You're a working screenwriter.

                    JOHN
I never wanted to be a writer. It was a way to
direct.

                  THERAPIST
Why do you want to make movies, John?

                    JOHN
I want to move people. It's why I loved Legos
as a kid. I want to create something and watch
the expression on their face when I show them
what I made. I want to make them feel
something.

                  THERAPIST
If you couldn't make movies, what would you
do?

                    JOHN
I've wanted to make movies since I was ten.

                    THERAPIST
        If you can't.

John thinks about this, long and hard. He looks down,
staring at his Therapist's bright candy colored socks,
then looks up and says under his breath -

                    JOHN
        I want to do what you're doing.

Silence. The Therapist looks confused, as if he didn't
hear correctly.

                    THERAPIST
        What?

                    JOHN
        If I can't do it for the masses, I'll do it one at a
        time. If I can't make movies, I want to be a
        therapist.

The Therapist thinks about this.

                    THERAPIST
        Then do it.

                    JOHN
        I'm a C student. I hate school. There's no way
        I'm going back. No. Fucking. Way.

Soon after this therapy session, I found myself in a
classroom. I was back in school, this time studying
psychology instead of film. I found my voice. I fought

my Pseudo Self. I stopped seeking approval and started living outside of self (my head). I began to embrace and share my story, not owning what wasn't mine. I exercised transparency.

In a Shotglass

To be transparent,

- Fight your Pseudo Self (live your truth).

- Live outside of self (get out of your head).

- Live in healthy time (in the here and now).

- Don't own it (let go).

- Live inside out (don't allow external objects to have power over you, express your feelings).

- Accept, embrace, and share your story (give instead of take).

Chapter Two

STANCE

Now that we've softened the soil, it's time to plant seeds. In Transparency, you are allowing yourself to be you. In Stance, you are not allowing anyone to take that away. Stance is building the framework for your new container. This isn't just about having boundaries. It's more than digging a moat around your castle. Stance means driving your stake. It's about having non-negotiables. Your stance will define your character.

Who Are You?

This was the question he screamed at me as I stared straight ahead, focusing on a clock as if I could make it go faster with my stare. My hands were gripping my seams and my mind was spinning for an answer. There was none. It was a question they knew we couldn't answer, which is why they asked it. I stated my name and what my parents did for a living. I didn't know what else to say. The House laughed as the Pledge Master stepped back in front of my face like he was going to spit. Instead he whispered *We don't care what your fucking dad does. He's not rushing our house. We want to know who you are.* That's when I let him have it. I replied *I'm a student.*

Note: I didn't know it at the time but joining a fraternity was when I first experienced the power of a safe container.

None of the pledges could answer that question. But the truth was that they couldn't either. Not many people can. Most of us define ourselves by what we do. Five years ago, if you asked me that question, I would have said *I am a screenwriter.* Today, if you asked me the same question, I would not say *I am a therapist.* That is what I do but that is not who I am. My answer is different now because back then I did not have Stance. Today I do. Who you are involves an exploration of your character. Character is formed from your stance. In order to have Stance, you must have non-negotiables.

When I was nineteen, there wasn't much I wasn't willing to negotiate. I would allow you to yell in my face, assassinate my character, and make me eat live goldfish. I would stand on the beach in the middle of the night for five hours, dig ditches in triple digit heat, and live in the garage eating nothing but hotdog wieners and peanuts for two weeks, in exchange for membership into the club. Of course, I have no interest in joining a fraternity today. But I also have non-negotiables.

I believe we negotiate too much. Our jobs, our relationships, our boundaries, our time, our passions, our health, and our happiness. Without non-negotiables, you are flimsy. You do not know who you are. If you don't know who you are, how will you know where you are going? You become a piece of drift wood floating in the ocean. You are lost and stagnant. You compromise yourself. You get into abusive relationships. You fall into depression. You begin to believe you are worthless. You become grayed out like the deleted program on your desktop. Your container is cracked.

What are the things you are not willing to negotiate in your life? For example, here are a few of mine.

I will do my best to be a good father.

My father is an alcoholic. This means at some point in his life his addiction stunted his emotional growth. He did an excellent job at providing the basic needs for his family like food, water, shelter, and designer clothes. But he did not provide much of an ear, empathy, or most importantly, presence. One day I asked him if I could buy a model plane from the next door neighbor, a pudgy man selling toys out of his garage. His "hobby shop" was stocked with three hundred dollar remote control cars and airplane models that required hundreds of intricate balsa wood pieces and a degree from M.I.T. But for an eleven year old with an obsession for Legos, it was just another play session and hopefully an excuse to spend some quality time with pops. He gave me the cash. I bought the plane. He glanced at it and laughed. He said there was no way I could build that thing. He went back to clipping his toenails and reading the "Korean Times". I started building. Three hours later, my dad was snoring and I was sitting in front of what looked like a pile of popsicle sticks glued together. My dad woke up before I had time to hide my failure. He shook his head and said, *I told you*. WE REMEMBER MOMENTS LIKE THESE. They form our beliefs. They are why I have the non-negotiable above.

I will not associate with anyone who assassinates my character.

John Gottman was the master at predicting divorce. He had a 94 percent accuracy rate. He wasn't concerned with how many times a couple fought but rather *how* they fought. Assassinating one's character was a sure sign the relationship was doomed.

If you assassinate one's character, you are not fighting fair. You are using a gun instead of gloves. Simply put, you are being a bully. Bullies react from fear. They are operating from a false self, one driven by ego and approval. This means they will not have the tools to support / encourage / promote your growth. Instead, they will ride your coat tails and bring you down so they can feel better about themselves. I have enough weight to carry. I do not need more dead weight.

I will do my best to make my partner feel beautiful.

In CrossFit, RX means prescribed. It's the recommended weight / standard for the workout. This is not raising the bar, it's the minimum requirement. Many do not RX because they are not physically able. That's understandable. But if you don't do it because you don't want to push yourself, that's called lazy. Everyone that CrossFits knows this. The coaches remind us daily.

In relationships, the RX I have set for myself is to do my best to make my partner feel beautiful. I have not done this in the past. It requires time and effort. I was lazy. Lazy is not acceptable to me anymore in whatever I do, including relationships. Being faithful and remembering birthdays is not enough. I don't just want to be great at work or in the box, I want to be a great boyfriend / husband. Making my girlfriend / wife feel beautiful is non-negotiable because it is my new RX.

I will walk with mirrors (not literally).

I believe that men walk with mirrors and boys do not. To walk with mirrors means to be aware of your defects and be willing to change them. I refuse to be a boy. I've been one for most of my life. Also, one cannot be transparent without self examination. Without Transparency, growth is almost impossible and growth is not something I am willing to negotiate.

I will have a cause.

I believe every man should have something they are fighting for. It doesn't have to be solving world hunger. It simply means having direction and a driving passion behind cause. Without direction, there's no journey. No mission. You're a lake, not an ocean. The ocean is where you find life.

A cause creates life.

I will not let my work determine my worth.

I used to determine my value by what I've accomplished. My value came in the form of a sale. At one point the value was selling scripts, then drinks (when I ran the family business). By defining my worth by what I sold, I sold myself. I became powerless. I was not human. I was a robot. It contributed to my unhappiness as well as the expiration of my marriage. I will never let that happen again.

I will take care of myself first.

I will not be able to help others if I cannot take care of myself. If I want to continue my cause - coaching others - I cannot negotiate my self care.

I will always have non-negotiables.

My non-negotiables are what make me who I am today. These are the things that define my character. They are what I'm not willing to negotiate about myself. They give me value, a spine, a shape to pour my transparency into.

Model in a Bottle Dot Com

People thought I was a pimp once. Literally. When I was in my late 20s, I had this idea to create an internet reality show about models. Nothing with nudity, just *real* working models in Los Angeles. Streaming video was just introduced to the world and there were no modeling shows on television at the time. This was pre Tyra Bank's "America's Top Model". But Modelinabottle failed miserably. It failed because I was negotiable. I had an investor who believed in me. He gave me $100K to launch it. I rented a million dollar penthouse on The Sunset Strip and gave six models free rent in exchange for the ability to document their lives, castings, photo shoots, daily routines at the penthouse, etc. They ended up walking all over me. Or more accurately, I allowed them to because I had no stance. The penthouse became a frat house. The models brought in their boyfriends and had parties. They ditched the camera and were never home to chat with fans. Eventually, the owner of the penthouse terminated the lease. She thought I was running a high class escort service.

Here's what I negotiated:

- My friendship. My investor was also a friend. He trusted me with his money and I negotiated it for approval from others.

- My relationships. I pressured my girlfriend at the time to ask her agency (she was also modeling at the time) to connect me with talent. By doing this, I was willing to negotiate her reputation and career, as well as our relationship.

- My character. Allowing the talent to not follow the rules and act inappropriately gave off the impression that the person behind this project - me - was filming an episode of "Girls Gone Wild." I was portrayed as a soft-core porn producer and I was willing to negotiate that for a chance to jump on the internet gold rush at the time.

- My gifts. Let's face it, I didn't go to film school to produce a modeling show. I did not have a genuine passion for the modeling business. I negotiated my talents for an image of success. In a nutshell, I sold out.

Would Modelinabottle.com have been a successful business if I had non-negotiables? I don't know. Ok, probably not. But I do know that I wasn't ready for success. I had no Stance. Success in that world would have only encouraged me to be more negotiable, which means getting further away from knowing who I am. With that kind of success and power, everything would be negotiable to me, including my friends, my family, and myself. I believe this happens to many lottery winners who do not have a Stance. When one doesn't have a Stance, they make decisions based on their Pseudo Self, not their Solid Self.

Having a stance strengthens your spine, which will protect you. Many fall into abusive relationships because they don't have non-negotiables. They allow themselves emotional and/or physical harm in the name of love.

Relationships mean compromise, not

compromising yourself.

By having non-negotiables, you are creating a shield. You are protecting yourself as well as your character. You are creating a safe container. In addiction, making an effort to not fall back into the cycle is called relapse prevention. In Stance, it's called relapse protection.

What are you negotiating in your life right now? With your relationships, parents, friends, boyfriend, yourself? What about at work? Do you have any non-negotiables?

Who are you?

Having a stance means having non-negotiables.

The Day I Didn't Fit In

This is the actual post from my blog the day I was terminated:

I feel scared, confused, and disposable. I want to believe that what happened today is a test to see how much I've grown. I want to believe things are meant. No what ifs, only what is. I feel like I'm on a balance beam, wind trying to shake me but I'm holding on tightly, not with my hands but only my stance. My legs are frozen, numb, in shock and I hope that I feel them soon. I trust that they will propel me forward. I feel that if I don't move forward, I am nothing. I am a lie, a puppet, a pumped out product with a generic label stamped on my forehead. The thought makes me feel nauseous and cheap. I left the house because I just had to go. Anywhere. I got on my motorcycle even though there is a chance of rain. Let it rain. Let it pour. It will make me feel alive. I need that tonight. I came to the nearest wifi coffee shop. I feel safe here, like it's the home base tree. I parked in a car space, then got back on my bike and rode up the sidewalk and parked right in front. Someone yelled "Fuck yeah". It made my heart smile. I felt like Batman inside my flat black helmet. I don't care. Give me a fucking ticket. This is me. I am here. Armed only with a computer stained with palm marks, I find a seat in the corner. Then I shrink. I've been here before, in this state of mind, one filled with desperation, a slippery well. My sweatshirt tightens and I feel dehydrated like I did years ago when I was writing screenplays in coffee shops all day. I take a sip of my warm coffee, wanting to rip out of my skin because this is a coffin and I can't do it again. I can't. I won't. This place is fucking lonely and miserable, a hamster wheel. Now I question everything. Maybe I'm spinning on one already and don't know it. Suddenly I am concerned about the rain, worried I'm going to get a ticket. I look down at my helmet and realize it's just a helmet. Then I look up to see that I got a note on this post. One note from a follower on my blog. It says You are not alone. These four words snap me back, reminding me it's different this time. There is no What ifs because I am not writing this to be someone. Only What is. I am writing this as someone. That is the difference. Suddenly I can feel my legs. They feel strong like the steel in my boots.

After working four years for a nonprofit organization, I was ecstatic when I was hired to be a program director of a private treatment center for eating disorders. This was a chance of a life time. It meant I would hire my own team of therapists and spearhead my own treatment center. It also meant yoga and a personal chef. It felt too good to be true. As it turns out, it was. After three weeks, they told me I "wasn't a good fit."

I was let go without explanation. The residential center I was supposed to run wasn't even up yet. I was *training* at one of the other treatment centers until my boss's licensing came through. Residential, outpatient, and transitional living were all owned by one person. She spent the last twenty-five years building her empire. I looked up to what she had accomplished, a well oiled machine pumping out treatment as if it came in cans on a factory belt. But I refuse to be a product, which I believe was the reason I was laid off.

I am disclosing this story to show you how Transparency and Stance works. So let's use my story as an example.

When someone gets let go or fired, the first feeling is usually one of panic. How am I going to pay my bills? Food? Rent? After logic kicks your ass, your emotional side takes over. You begin to internalize what happened. You begin labeling yourself. *Maybe I'm not good enough. Maybe I deserve to be fired. Maybe I should find a new career? I am worthless. I am stupid.*

But if you've worked your transparency muscles, you will:

- Fight your Pseudo Self. (live your truth)

All the thoughts that are labeling you as worthless, stupid, or incompetent, are from your Pseudo Self. You realize this and fight it. You acccpt that the event has made you sad, which is fair, but being let go does not define your worth.

- Live outside of self (get out of your head).

You will not let your mind / thoughts drive you into the ground. You will allow yourself to be sad for the loss, but not dwell, obsess, or fall into the quicksand.

- Live in healthy time (in the here and now).

You will not think about the past, reviewing all the days you worked there and what you *could have, should have done.* Or worry about the future. What am I going to do now? How am I going to pay my bills? What are my friends going to think of me? Instead, you will live in the here and now. Accept what you feel and be present in it. If you need to cry, cry. If you need to yell, scream, throw a chair, so be it. This is how you feel. This is where you are. For me, I needed to park my motorcycle on the sidewalk and blog.

- Don't own it (your experiences / events are not yours to control).

You will choose to believe that you were meant to be at that job for the exact amount of time that you were. Like a pair of bowling shoes, that job was borrowed and it was time to return it for someone else to learn from.

- Share your story (give instead of take).

One day you will be able to use this story as ammunition to help someone with what they are going through. This memory becomes another bullet in your chamber.

Scroll through your non-negotiables. One of mine helped me reframe the situation almost instantly, lifting anxiety right off my shoulders as if it was on wires.

One of my non-negotiables:

I will not work for anyone who doesn't allow me to be me and / or doesn't respect me or my gifts.

I don't want work to be a factory; I want it to be a canvas. I want to paint. Invent. Create. She did not allow that. That is non-negotiable for me. Also, the way she let me go demonstrated her lack of respect for me, as a clinician and a person. Also, non-negotiable.

Once I realized that by working there I would be negotiating myself, there was nothing to be upset about. It was either have a cushy job with great pay and run my own treatment center but live with a cracked container, or be temporarily unemployed but live in a safe container. Hands down, I chose the later. The job would not have allowed me to grow, but instead would have turned me into a robot. Having a safe container would encourage growth and the opportunity to share my gifts with the world. Maybe have my own treatment center one day. Do those two options even compare? Of course not. At that moment, I as almost relieved she let me go. That it meant it saved me a difficult conversation about how I didn't feel like I fit into her company.

The difference between dignity and pride is that one stems from ego, the other from your Stance.

True Story.

FADE IN:

INT. CHINESE RESTAURANT - NIGHT

JOHN sits by the window alone reading "Linchpin" as he finishes his last dim sum when the WAITRESS approaches.

                    WAITRESS
          How're you doing?

John looks up at her, deadpan.

                    JOHN
          You know what?

She instantly looks nervous.
                    JOHN
          You've been asking people that all day. So
          maybe I should ask you how you're doing?

She looks a bit shocked, confused, taken back. She
fumbles her words...

                    WAITRESS
          Ummm... fine, tired. Been here since 10 am. I
          can't wait to go home.

                    JOHN
          I bet.

She smiles.

                    WAITRESS
          Thank you.

She needed that.

                    JOHN
          You're welcome.

                    WAITRESS
                  (extra friendly)
          Would you like anything else?

JOHN
No, I'm good. Just the check. Thank you.

She grabs the check from her apron, sets it on the table with a fortune cookie on top, smiles, and leaves.

John grabs the fortune cookie and cracks it. He reads his fortune, looks out the window.

His eyes get glassy.

He really needed that, especially this week since he was let go from his job.

He turns back at the fortune, snaps a picture of it with his phone.

FADE OUT:

Perspective changes everything. You can feel hopeless and discouraged one minute then hopeful and blessed the next just by changing your perspective. A simple example of this is when we see or hear about a great tragedy. 911, the flood in New Orleans, the earthquake that swallowed Japan. Suddenly, him leaving his socks on the couch isn't that big of a deal. Your boss is tolerable. The bills are just bills. At least you have your health. Only your perspective shifted.

Stance can help change perspective. This means once you have your Stance, you have new lenses to look through. You have another tool under your belt. Stances don't have to be huge life altering non-negotiables. They can be simple, fun, something you hold on to just for you.

For example,

Fuck It Friday!

For me, this means a donut. I have a weakness for them. I know they are bad for me. But every Friday I allow myself one. The Stance isn't the fried dough drenched in sugar. It's allowing myself a treat every once in a while, telling myself that everything doesn't have to be black or white, cut and dry. Rewards are okay. I can fudge. As a matter of fact, I must. It's healthy.

It doesn't matter if it's food. An experience. A massage. A workshop. A trip. An affirmation. A compliment. A day off? You need it. Not the reward; the ability to give yourself something you deserve without feeling guilt. The process of allowing yourself to receive is crucial. You are validating your worth. Many struggle with this. Instead, they focus solely on others for validation. Having a stance means to learn how to validate yourself. This is a tool. An important tool when you begin to build yourself a safe container.

Having a stance also means taking back what you've lost. Knitting, skating, writing, jumping on trampolines. What used to make you forget? What brought you joy? Take it back. Through the grind of life, so many of us lose what once made us happy. It becomes the project car sitting on blocks and collecting dust in the garage. It's time to take the cover off and get back to building, discovering, learning, creating - whatever it was that made you lose track of time.

For me, it wasn't writing screenplays. It was the process of giving birth to ideas. It started in childhood while building with Legos. I used to lock myself in the room for hours and get lost in my creations. It's always been there. After I quit screenwriting, I lost that part of me. I stopped conceiving and a piece of me died.

Take It Back

I stopped going to coffee shops after I quit screenwriting. This was the actual blog post the day I stepped back into one to write again:

"Surf your balls off" she replies casually as if she's reminding me my shoes are untied. I chuckle on the inside as I plop down at my table and punch those exact words into the passcode box for free wireless. I am back in the corner of a coffee shop today. This time, answering client emails and questions from my blog, hoping to ignite a change in the way one thinks. Everything's the same. The cheap coffee, the bad art, the starlet whipping foam mechanically behind the counter, and the sea of struggling screenwriters typing with urgency which will only last a few minutes before they too become robots. I guess the only difference between now and five years ago, besides the amount of grays in my hair and change in my pocket, is who I'm typing for. Before, it was for me, my life, my future. Now, it's for others, their life, and their future. I am not saying I have the ability to help anyone. I am just saying that is my intent. I ponder this and realize that this small difference, the intent to do something for someone else instead of yourself, creates a bulletproof sense of productivity because you can't fail when you give. They may still

not like what I have to say, but they can't argue with my heart. I am still writing on spec as they say in Hollywood. Before, the speculation that my story is viable. Today, the speculation that your story is valuable. This makes me happy. I take a deep breath and smile, angled on a wooden chair with my back against the wall like I used to sit for hours years ago, realizing that I can take this place back. I feel comfortable here. I feel safe. It's my treehouse.

It wasn't until I started a blog that I began to take things back. I didn't realize it at the time. I didn't say to myself, *I need to take things back that I once loved doing.* I created a blog because I wanted to connect. But inside the itch to create was surfacing again. The blog just happened to be the tool I used. Creating allowed me to connect, not only with others, but with myself. That is the important piece. What ever you decide to take back will allow you –to connect with yourself.

Unlock Your Inner Code

Carl Jung called it the *Divine Child*, Emmet Fox called it the *Wonder Child*, Charles Whitfield called it the *Child Within*. I call it the Inner Code. I don't see that part of you as a c*hild*. I see it as your core, which your daily *adult*, work, relationships, bills, gym, dishes, and deadlines has stuffed into a box and locked away. What's keeping it trapped is fear. You are afraid that by unlocking your inner code, you will not be what you *should* be, who you *should* be. Unlocking it means being different and being different is scary. But the truth is you will never be who you were meant to be if you don't unlock your inner code.

You have muted what originally made you unique. You have turned a snowflake into a snowball. In order to be your true self, to tip your potential, to release that part of you which is ultimately alive, you must unlock your Inner Code. Rip off that muzzle you strapped on yourself years ago.

Find the right combination to the lock that's keeping you from who you really are. Growth isn't always about change. Sometimes it's about a reunion. A reunion with yourself. Explore what you gravitate toward and rediscover what moves you. You can't move forward, evolve, and grow, if you don't allow yourself to flourish. Find the spirit you were born with. Open the lock.

Having a stance means taking things back by unlocking your code.

Bright Spots

Someone once told me *Life is shit except for a few moments of joy.* If that's the case, we must stretch those moments like cookie dough. Everyone has bright spots, though most are unaware of them. We are so busy obsessing about the future and dwelling on the past that we don't notice them. They fly by like our adolescence. Turn your dial from macro to micro and taste the nectar in your life. The first sip of hot coffee in the morning. The few seconds after a brisk run. Consuming your favorite meal. The scent of your lover. A life changing conversation. Feeling beautiful in a dress. The moment you forget you're on a motorcycle.

The more you are aware of your bright spots, the more you're training your brain to appreciate the little things in life. If we stretch these moments and string them together, your days will feel happier, lighter, and you can flip the script and believe that . . .

Life is joy except for a few moments of shit.

Being aware of your bright spots and stretching them is having a stance.

Be Heard

The way to be heard is to express yourself. Many hold in their feelings because they don't want to rock the boat. This turns into resentment and manifests in unhealthy ways. Your feelings are like a pressure cooker. You must release the valve. It requires tools to do this in a healthy way. The more transparent you are, according to my definition of Transparency, the easier it will be release this valve.

One would think self expression would fall into the Transparency stage. Although the act of telling someone how you feel is a form of transparency, what's really happening is you are allowing yourself to be heard. Not just to others but more importantly to yourself. And that's the most important piece, being heard for you. Not them. You are giving yourself a voice, proving to yourself that you exist. This process forces you to listen to you. Many people don't listen to themselves. They have an inner dialogue but they are not heard. If you are not heard, you become invisible. You are not there. Or are you? This can't be a question. Put your hand down. Instead, stand. Speak. Teach. Take over the class. It is imperative to do this, not only in intimate relationships but across the board in all your relationships. To your friends, family, boss, co-workers. Stating your position, even an emotional one, is part of your stance.

Having a stance means being heard.

In a Shotglass

To create your Stance, you must

- Have non-negotiables (things you are not willing to negotiate about yourself).

- Take things back / Unlock your Inner Code (allow yourself to enjoy what truly makes you happy).

- Stretch your bright spots (enjoy more of the little things that bring you joy throughout the day).

- Be Heard (listen to you by expressing yourself).

Chapter Three

CONTAINER

I believe our emotional state, like our bodies, has the ability to heal itself as long as you provide it a safe container. I believe we prevent healing by creating an unhealthy space, one that invites harm. We fall into the same dysfunctional patterns, retreat to our unhealthy coping habits, and get stuck in a suffering cycle. It's like cutting yourself over and over again on the same spot. Creating a safe container is like applying pain relieving cream and a bandage.

But healing doesn't come without work. You have to choose to work on yourself while you are in that "safe container." This is how therapy works. A therapist provides a safe space. In this space growth happens. Of course "treatment" requires more than just a safe space. But you don't necessarily need a therapist to grow. I believe a therapist can expedite your growth, but one is not required in order to change. You can create your own space for change. The way you do this is by building a safe container. We can build our own. We can rebuild ourselves through others.

My Treatment

My definition of *therapist* used to be someone who looked like Dr. Drew, decked out in a freshly pressed shirt and nursing a Chai Latte with one hand and a leather steering wheel with the other as he swings into a private treatment center somewhere in Malibu.

You can imagine my resistance when I accepted a job as an addiction counselor working with underprivileged teenagers in Los Angeles. I had to wear a uniform, khaki pants and a golf shirt. I was also required to obtain a class B license in order to drive a 16 passenger van for Friday outings. I felt more like a camp counselor than a therapist. To top it off, the treatment model was Therapeutic Community. They never taught us *Therapeutic Community* in grad school. It wasn't on the curriculum. It sounded old, from back in the day. And as it turns out, it was.

The idea of people helping people dates back to the 1800s. It is the core of 12 step meetings, correctional facilities, group homes, rehabs, and even fraternities. All these are safe containers that promote growth. The Therapeutic Community believes that people can change and creates an environment that helps to facilitate change. The Therapeutic Community allows a person to grow by fostering an environment where people are valued and accepted. A strong sense of belonging to a nurturing community in an atmosphere of trust and security is a central tenet of The Therapeutic Community.

Then what did they need me for? That was the broken record playing in my head for the first six months as I begrudgingly drove to the dilapidated two bedroom house that was rumored to be haunted. I was confused and frustrated. I nearly quit. Many times. But what kept me there were the kids and their stories. Rape, drugs, self mutilation, suicidal attempts, 16-year-olds that had no desire to live anymore. Some were mandated into therapy by court, others literally had nowhere else to go. They were booted from foster care or had parents that wanted to pass them like batons. But they all had something in common besides their struggles with substance abuse: fatherless homes. Their dads were out of the house or out of their minds. Most of the kids did not even know their fathers. Some fathers were in prison. Being "older" and one of the only male therapists there, I felt how thirsty they were for a positive male role model, a man who didn't want anything from them. The girls were standing too close. The boys were imitating me. If I didn't have a stance (non-negotiables), I would have left. But one of my non-negotiables is to be a good father one day. I knew in my heart that this would be the ultimate training ground. So I stayed. For the next four years, I would cook, play, laugh, cry, *do* life with these kids. I was completely oblivious to the fact that *I* was the one in treatment.

There is no doubt that the Therapeutic Community model works. AA alone has over two million members. CrossFit boxes are changing lives daily. There is a difference between a CrossFit box and a commercial gym. One is a safe container. The other is not. A CrossFit box provides a space that allows members to get into each others' lives, support weaknesses, and challenge false beliefs. It promotes growth. It's a therapeutic community. A commercial gym does not provide this kind of space. Members check in, workout alone, and leave. The pledging programs in fraternities and sororities are designed for pledges to grow stronger together so that when they become brothers and sisters, the house stays tight. Police academies, fire departments, the military, CrossFit boxes, are all safe containers that change lives daily.

So the question is, can you microbrew this model and apply it to yourself in everyday life? I believe the answer is yes or I wouldn't have written this book. It wasn't my work in residential that cemented this theory. It was building a new safe container for myself after my divorce that proved anyone could build a new container.

Building a safe container starts with:

Structure

Structure doesn't mean going to work, hitting the gym, eating dinner, watching TV, and going to sleep. That's called a schedule. Structure is not a routine. It's a framework that keeps you balanced. People tend to focus solely on work and the relationship they are in and live lopsided lives.

Structure stretches you. It's the foundation of any safe container. The kids I was treating in residential ended up there because they did not have the tools to create a solid structure. But you do. Here's a good way to think about your structure.

Self Care Plan

There are six basic needs: Emotional, Spiritual, Sexual, Financial, Physical, and Intellectual. This is your Self Care Plan. When you meet these needs, you are taking

care of yourself and you must take care of yourself if
you want to build a safe container.

Let's start with Emotional. Everyone needs a space to
vent and process. For some, this space is created
through friends and family. For others, a bathtub and a
crossword puzzle, coffee and conversation, a power bar
and a CrossFit box, a webcam and a therapist. Many
do life without this space and end up turning to drugs,
alcohol, sex, food, so many things used to numb or
cope with feelings.

Spiritual. This doesn't mean you have to attend church.
It just means you believe in something bigger than you.
Having this mindset allows for surrender / acceptance,
and helps with letting go. Sometimes our ego acts as a
barrier to healing. If you believe you are a part of
something instead of the whole, the ego shrinks. It's
much easier to "lose" when you're on a team than if
you're playing solo.

How do you fulfill your spiritual needs? What do you
do / where do you go to connect with something
greater than you? The more you have a relationship
with this greater power / energy, the more power /
energy you will have with your "problems."

Yoga
Prayer
Surfing

Physical. Many don't believe physical activity is a need.
I believe it's imperative when it comes to a healthy
happy life. It's a natural way to reduce stress and build

self esteem. We are not meant to sit in cubicles all day. We used to hunt our own food. Swim. Run. Play. Build things with our bare hands. Today we spend most of our lives in bubbles, cars, offices, elevators, homes, and mostly our heads. Our bodies become weak and we start to feel old. We don't realize we're deteriorating. Physical activity is not just about looking a certain way. It rejuvenates our body and breathes life into our lungs. It gives us a sense of empowerment. We feel better about ourselves. It's the fastest way to raise self esteem. And it doesn't matter what the activity is, we just need to sweat every single day. We need it like water and sun. Yes, physical activity is a need. If you don't have a form of it in your life, your life is unbalanced.

Paleo Diet
Running
Surfing
CrossFit

As you can see, some may bleed into others. That's okay. For me CrossFit can go under both my physical and sexual needs.

Sexual. Sexual needs don't just mean sex. It's fulfilling a need to feel sexy, attractive, and confident. A new dress. Salsa dancing. A motorcycle. These can all fall under the sexual needs category. We are sexual beings. If you deny that, you are losing a part of your truth. Feeling sexy is an extremely powerful feeling. We need to feed it.

Financial.

Intellectual.

Once you have a Self Care Plan, you will see what needs aren't being fulfilled and which are overloaded. It will be a blue print on how to start building structure to balance your needs.

Your new structure should be designed to accommodate the needs that are not being fulfilled and taking some time away from the ones you are spending too much time on. For many, this will be their financial need - work. I think we focus so much on our careers, we forget about the rest of us. WE ARE NOT WHAT WE DO.

Here's my current self-care plan.

Emotional

Therapist (once a week)
Self help books (one book a week)
Friends (a few times a week)
Girlfriend (daily)
Blogging (daily)
Riding motorcycle (weekends)

Intellectual

Books
Other people's blogs

Spiritual

Prayer (daily)

Physical

CrossFit (daily)
Healthy diet (daily)
- Currently no health or dental insurance.

Financial

Webcam sessions but don't have a secure job.

Sexual

CrossFit (daily)
Girlfriend (daily)
Masturbation (as needed)
Riding motorcycle (weekends)

As you can see, my self-care is emotionally heavy. It's lacking in the financial, spiritual, and intellectual department.

Once you have a structure, it's time to implement a . . .

Program

In residential treatment, without a program it's just four walls and a roof. Structure is your blueprint. Running a program will be you building what you've designed.

Using my self-care plan above, here are some questions I would ask myself to start implementing a program.

What are the barriers getting in the way of fulfilling my financial needs?

I don't want to go back to a 9 to 5.
Busy trying to build a virtual practice.
Writing this book.
Blogging.

In the next month, give me a date that you will make a step toward fulfilling your financial need. And what is the action?

March 15. I will work on my resume and start looking online for therapist positions to possibly consider.

What are the barriers getting in the way of fulfilling your intellectual needs?

Time.
Laziness.
Not forced to attend workshops and seminars since I am not currently working at an agency.

In the next month, give me a date when you will take a step toward fulfilling your intellectual needs? And what is the action?

March 20. I will look up some free workshops and seminars. From that day on, I will wake up 30 mins earlier and read something online to educate myself on various topics.

What are the barriers getting in the way of fulfilling your spiritual needs?

The church I used to attend brings back memories of my ex-wife.
Laziness.
Don't want to drive 20 minutes.

In the next month, give me a date when you will take a step toward fulfilling your spiritual needs? And what is the action?

April 10. I will attend one house church in my area.

This would just be the beginning of a program. Depending on what works for you, you can get more into detail or pull back.

Write it down. Paint your bedroom wall with chalk paint and scribble it on your entire wall so you can see it everyday.

Program is all about action/ execution. Remember, growth is 50 percent revelations and 50 percent execution. We can process and have revelations all day. But without a program, growth and change are just ideas. It's like a car without an engine. You won't go anywhere. You will not reach your destination without running a program. Everyone's program will be different. You have to decide what yours will look like. Start small and focused. Pick one thing that you know you want to work on. Maybe it's your fitness and diet. Maybe it's learning to be a better listener. Maybe it's writing. Maybe exploring your passions. You've had this conversation with yourself before, haven't you?

What stopped you? Most likely fear. Go back to your non-negotiables. Maybe you can add one more.

You will not allow fear to stop you from growing.

Once you have a program, tell people about it. Announce your change. Put it out there. Most people keep it to themselves and there's no one to make them accountable. Tell your top five.

Now practice transparency and strengthen your stance daily and you will have three pistons pumping. If you've made it this far, it means you believe you are valuable and worth change. For most of us, getting to this point is the hardest part. Once you are here, results (more energy, less stress, generally happier mood) will fuel you to the next level.

Emotional Recycling

I am not referring to this in a literal sense. By emotional recycling I mean taking ownership and responsibility of your emotions. It is a crucial piece in building your final piston, your container.

I believe many relationships expire because we don't take ownership of our actions / words. This piles and piles until it's just better to dump the house instead of trying to rebuild it. If you don't own, you will foreclose. By not taking responsibility for your piece, you are encouraging a pissing contest. It doesn't matter how mature we appear, we can all be childish. We all have an ego. The five year old in us rears its bratty head and wants to play tit for tat. Note: This is not your Inner Child. It's your insecure, immature Pseudo Self. Suddenly, you are playing a game of tug of war and it's not about compromise, it's about winning. This mindset destroys relationships.

Remember, whenever you are taking instead of giving, closing instead of opening, you are living in Pseudo Self. That is not the true you. That behavior is your shield; you are hiding. This is why it's imperative to exercise your transparency muscles. The stronger they are, the easier it will be to take ownership. By being emotionally responsible, you are giving. You are contributing to decreasing pain in this world. You are recycling and it will make you feel good about yourself.

If you have difficulty taking ownership, I want you to think of it this way: Say you're driving and you see someone throw trash out the window. Not gum, but an entire bag of fast food. What do you think about this person that just littered? It's offensive, isn't it? We have to share this planet and he's being extremely inconsiderate of others. Would you want to hang out with this person? Is this the kind of person you want your kids around? When you don't take emotional responsibility, you are being *that* guy. Or girl. It's simple. If everyone recycled, the world would be a cleaner place. That is a fact. If everyone took ownership of how they treated others, there would be less pain in the world. That is a fact.

Why is emotional recycling (taking ownership) important in building our container? Taking ownership protects us. When you take responsibility of your words and actions, you will gravitate toward others that do the same. Taking ownership is a belief, a movement, a stance. So it acts as a protectant, a radar. You will be less attracted to that "hot guy" if he is emotionally irresponsible. You will protect yourself from a dysfunctional relationship. Your patience for friends that just verbally vomit on you will grow thin. Your choice creates clusters, tribes of people with the same mission. You will begin to surround yourself with people that promote growth. This process means you're building your container.

Use Your Ego

First, you believe that taking ownership is less about the other person and more about you. Why not use your ego to help you take ownership. The process of owning your faults means two things: you're aware of what doesn't work and what you would like to change. The act of owning means you are actually doing work on yourself, bettering yourself, gaining.

Taking ownership is one of the most powerful tools you have in an argument. People don't realize this. When you take ownership, you instantly defuse. It's an extinguisher. Aikido is a martial art where you take the other person's force and use it against them. For example, instead of striking back, you would use the force of your opponent's swing to throw them over your shoulder. This is what you are doing when you take ownership. They can't argue with something you just owned. There is no fight. Then it gives them a chance to own their piece. Taking ownership is contagious. When someone takes ownership for their actions, especially someone you are intimate with, you can't help but to reflect on yourself and think what things you could / should take ownership on. The best way to get someone to own something is to take ownership yourself. Even if they don't actually do it, your action will cause a reaction in them, to reflect, ponder, question, and hopefully own. It might take them a while to react. If they do, there is resolution and this experience will make you closer, the relationship will grow stronger. If they don't, you will still feel good about; one, stopping the fight, and two, doing your piece to contribute to a healthy relationship.

Your Top Five

A few years ago, a cell phone company did a promotion where you could add your top five friends to your plan. The slogan was *Who's in your top five?* I remember the five mugs circulating on the cell phone screen. I remember it because it made me question who would be in my *Top Five.*

I didn't have many friends when I was married. I had a lot of acquaintances, because I was running a scenic restaurant bar in Hollywood. Actors, producers, screenwriters, DJs, bartenders, door guys, I was surrounded by people all the time. But none of them were friends, according to my definition of *friend* today. They were part of my social network and I spent a lot of time with them. However, they did not contribute to my truth. Under the "friendship," there was a negotiation, an exchange. It was not announced. It was subconscious. I received approval and affirmation and they received entrance into a club, a pay check, free meals, and my approval and affirmation. We became a group of followers, a school of fish swimming in a bowl.

Here's what happens: In high school, we can't be picky. Literally. We don't have the tools. We are just discovering who we are. There's no way of knowing who will contribute to our growth because we don't know what growth looks like. Combine that with the force of peer pressure and our natural desire for acceptance and approval at that age and friends become labels, how we identify ourselves. Skaters, cheerleaders, jocks, band geeks, gangsters. This is the social model that sets us up for life. According to Erik Erikson's Stages of Development, our basic strengths at this age are devotion and fidelity. Instead of finding ourselves in friends, we lose ourselves in them. Then, in college, we start to form beliefs. We have ideas, opinions, and choices. Now we're able to give instead of take. We have tools to start looking for mutual, satisfying relationships. This means we can slowly peel our labels off. Or at least there's an opportunity for that. For many, it's make up time, a chance to redeem what they missed out on in high school. Now that we've blossomed, we can be the prom kings and queens. And this is where the road forks. If that "make up time" never gets made up here, meaning we don't get our crown and realize it's made of plastic, it carries on into our twenties. I believe this is when our Pseudo Self is the strongest. We posture, perform, desperately try to prove ourselves to others. There is a danger in this. We drift further from our Solid Self. We try to redo instead of reinvent. This keeps us from finding our *Top Five*, friends that will make us the best version of us.

Now, if you fall in love and get married in your twenties, your picket fence takes you down another road. Priorities get rearranged and you only have so much spare time. Your Pseudo Self clips your friends as if they were expired coupons. It tells you that all you need to be happy is your wife. Friends are extra. They become a spare, like the tire in your trunk. This is when you fall into codependency. You and your wife become enmeshed. You begin to live one life instead of two. Everything goes through the other person. Schedules, plans, money. You lose yourself in the relationship. This stunts personal growth, which means your container is cracked.

We must be aware of what may be preventing our growth. Back to transparency muscles . . . the stronger they are, the easier it is to shed labels, de-mesh from our lovers, attract friends that will call you out on your shit, support your strengths, challenge you, and accept you, completely.

You can't build a safe container by yourself or just with your partner. Like any therapeutic community, you are rebuilding yourself through others. Finding your Top Five is a crucial piece in building your new container.

Gregslist

I was on Craigslist looking for a roommate because my wife and I decided we needed a separation. My new roommate was Greg, a single white gay male with exquisite taste in living space. I can feel his proud smile as I am typing this. A few months in, my wife and I decided to divorce. This left me with a roommate but no friends. My wife was my only friend, which I believe was a contributing factor to our expiration.

I was in my mid-30s and found myself having to start over again. But it would not be easy this time. I had nothing to offer anyone. The club was gone. The connections were gone. All that was left was a very broken boy in his 30s. The good news, which I would not discover until later, was that not having anything to offer but myself was an excellent filter to catch real friends. I guess you can say Greg was a friend. But I didn't feel like I was on his list. I felt like he kept me from his other friends. I felt that high school thing happening again and, just coming from the club world - the biggest high school of all, I found myself looking elsewhere. My search might have hurt his feelings and if you're reading this Greg, now you know it was me, not you.

So I met a friend at church, the first Asian guy I've ever met that can actually grow a full beard. He was burly and crass, just like me. He introduced me to another friend, another Asian guy in his 30s, divorced, and studying to be a therapist. The similarities were uncanny. He was a newscaster. I was a screenwriter. We both felt like we were chasing the wrong rainbow and quit to become therapists. It was like God said, *Hey John, I know you've never had any Asian friends. So let me give you a Chinese version of yourself.* Sam and I became roommates. Through Sam, I met another friend, my Spiritual brother. Through him I met a half Chinese / Hungarian guy with the same simian palm lines as me going through a similar rebirth. That was freaky. Then

I met another, a war vet adjusting to life back in the states. I called him my same size brother because he was exactly the same height and build.

Suddenly, I had a core, all broken men in their 30's, trying to figure out life. These people were very different than the type of people I was used to spending time with. They weren't actors, models, or club promoters. They were just normal guys and we had nothing to offer each other except our stories. So we began to do life together. Big Bear, coffee shops, CrossFit, mountain bikes, walks around the lake, movies, dinners. We challenged and sharpened each other.

They encouraged me to write again. I opened up Final Draft after five years and wrote a screenplay about my experiences with them. This script wasn't to sell, it was just for me. It was a way to unlock my code, to create again. My friends enjoyed the script and encouraged me to go out and make it. With their support, we began raising money to make it independently. Meanwhile, the producer of the project encouraged me to create some silly videos on the internet as a marketing tool. That when I created *The Angry Therapist*.

To this day, my phone lights up "Super Size Brother, Simian Brother, Spiritual Brother, and Same Size Brother" when they call. My top five.

We are not meant to do life alone, and just because you have a boyfriend / girlfriend / husband / wife doesn't mean you're not alone. We all need our own set of friends, whether we're in a relationship or not. We are inherently social creatures, meant to learn from each other and strengthen each other. Without solid healthy friends, we become dull swords. The weapon we fight life with becomes minimal.

It's time to put your friends in a strainer and spend more time with the ones that are going to encourage growth, not stunt it.

Strainer

- Friends that accept you and all your defects.
- Friends that believe in / support your journey.
- Friends that practice transparency.
- Friends that have a stance.
- Friends that see you as a part of *their* container.

The weaker your transparency muscles and the less stance you have, the more you will attract and be attracted to false friends. This is because you are operating from Pseudo Self (false self), not Solid Self (true self). This is why Transparency and Stance come first. The soil must be soft and seeds must be planted. The more work you put into Transparency and Stance, the tighter your strainer, which means the more you will attract people that will encourage your growth, your path, your truth.

The Other F Word

We've talked about friends and lovers. Now let's talk briefly about family. The first thing to remember is that you cannot change your family. It's wasted energy.

Don't even try. Instead, focus solely on being your Solid Self when you are interacting with your family members. Be Solid at all times, on the phone, email, text, and in person. This means being transparent and holding on to your stance. This will be extremely difficult. There will be an internal tug of war between what you were and who you want to be. When you are around your family, you will snap back into the same family dynamics you grew up with up. This is why grown men, CEOs of giant corporations, regress into insecure teenagers when they're around their mothers.

Kickstands

One dysfunctional behavior common in many families is using one member as what I call a *kickstand*. Whenever two family members have a problem with each other, one or both will bring in a third member. They will respond to anxiety between each other by shifting the focus to this third member. Two are on the inside and one is on the outside. For example, rather than mom confronting dad about her frustration with him, she will vent on her son. In doing so, she will pass the anxiety on to her son. This process allows space for character assassination. Mom will be speaking from years of hurt and anger. Simply put, this is when family members talk shit about each other. It also puts the son in an unfair position. If the son allows this behavior, mom will continue. She will depend on this process every time she has conflict with her husband. This creates cracks in the family container.

Don't be a kickstand.

If all family members refuse to be kickstands, the person with the conflict will be forced to resolve their issues on their own. They will have to express themselves to the person they have a conflict with. This means they will be forced to exercise transparency muscles and create their stance. By not being a kickstand, you are giving them tools to build their own safe container as well as a safe container for the family. Remember this. Let it be the motivating factor to stay firm in your decision.

If you live your truth around your family, live in Solid Self and refuse to be a kickstand, the family dynamic will change. This is not psychology. It's physics. For every action, there's a reaction. Most likely their reaction will come in the form of resistance. You are tipping the boat. They are afraid to fall into the water. Don't mistake that as them not loving you. They will adjust; it just takes time. Be patient. Remember, your focus is not to change them. Your goal is just to live the truest version of you. By doing this, you will shift your family dynamic. This creates a space for change. Hopefully, your change will ignite change in others. This is the same concept used in a therapeutic community. It can also be applied to your family. Living in your Solid Self around your family may be the most difficult piece in building your new container. It requires a tremendous amount of courage and strength. You're shaking a foundation, cracking concrete. The amount of work you do in Transparency and Stance will determine whether you use a jackhammer or a toothpick.

In a Shotglass

To create your container, you must

- Have a structure (not a schedule, a program based around a self care plan).

- Create your Top Five (friends that will make you the best version of you. Use your strainer).

- Stay Solid around your family (be transparent, hold on to your stance, and don't be a kickstand).

Conclusion

Practicing transparency and having a stance, continuously in your life, everyday of your life, gives you tools. Once you have these tools, you can build a safe container for yourself. And in this safe container, you will grow.

As you grow, you will be able to be more transparent and have a stronger stance which = a safer container = even more transparency and even a stronger stance = safer container = more growth.

It's a cycle. The trick is to keep this cycle going, keep pedaling on that bike. This momentum will keep you stable through life and the everyday obstacles you face daily.

People buy self help books because they are looking for a magic answer. I am here to tell you that there is no magic answer. But I am also here to tell you that growth isn't as complicated as it seems.

Be transparent. Create your stance.

Build your container.

That's it. If you just focus on these, you will grow. I promise. I know because I have used this method with my clients as well as in my own life.

What Makes This Book Different Than Any Other Self Help Book

This book is not an intervention. It is an invitation. I have built you a safe container online, a virtual therapeutic community known as *The Angry Therapist*. It's a place where you can exercise your transparency muscles and rebuild yourself through others no matter where you are in the world. And it doesn't matter what you're going through, an expired relationship. It's all about living a better life. If you are reading this book, you are invited.

I hope to see you inside.

  - Angry

www.theangrytherapist.com

ABOUT THE AUTHOR

My name is John Kim and I am a licensed Marriage Family Therapist. In 2010, I started a blog. Partly to document my own journey but also to create a dialogue that may help others. Coaching people online was not my intent but by the end of that year, I had two clients. By the end of the second year, I had coached over 100 people from all over the globe, treating individuals, couples, and facilitating groups - all this from my computer. Due to the overwhelming response, I quit my 9 to 5 and opened a "public" practice. I define my practice as "public" because I do everything online, including individual sessions, couples, and group work using Google Hangouts.

Today, *The Angry Therapist* is not just a blog / practice, it's a therapeutic community. It's a place for you to rebuild yourself through others. Inside, you'll find discussion forums on relationships, dating, love, career, life, as well as live online groups you can participate in from the convenience of your home.

The Angry Therapist a multi-platform brand intersecting technology and therapy. Through a suite of technology tools, my intent is to revolutionize the therapy and mental health industry, serving as an example of how technology can expand the reach of therapist practice, and help the industry learn how it can better treat more people through use of similar tools.

My goal is for you to have support in your pocket.

Made in the USA
San Bernardino, CA
11 December 2013